KIDS ENCYCLOPEDIA
SUPERFOOD

Your Tasty Adventures...

CONTENTS

 **HIGH FIBER**

 **NUTS:** Just a handful can keep you full and give you energy for hours!

1. **Introduction**
   - What Are Superfoods?
   - Why Are They Important for You?
2. **Superfood Categories**
   - Fruits
     - Blueberries, Strawberries, Avocados
     - Fun Facts: Why Are Blueberries Called Brain Berries?
     - Simple Recipes: Berry Smoothie
   - Vegetables
     - Spinach, Kale, Sweet Potatoes, Carrots
     - Fun Facts: What Makes Carrots Good for Your Eyes?
     - Simple Recipes: Spinach Omelet

 **HIGH PROTEIN SOURCE**

CHIA SEEDS: 2 tablespoons have almost as much calcium as a cup of milk.

- Grains and Seeds
    - Quinoa, Chia Seeds, Oats
    - Fun Facts: Why Are Chia Seeds a Super Seed?
    - Simple Recipes: Quinoa Salad
- Proteins
    - Salmon, Chicken, Nuts
    - Fun Facts: How Does Salmon Help Your Brain?
    - Simple Recipes: Chicken Wrap

ALWAYS READ THE MESSAGE IN BOTTLE, LOCATE IT DOWN!

WHAT ARE SUPERFOODS?

Superfoods are special types of foods that are very good for your body because they are packed with lots of important nutrients. These nutrients help you grow strong, stay healthy, and have lots of energy to play and learn. Think of superfoods like the superheroes of the food world – they have extra powers to keep you healthy!

HERE COMES THE ARMY OF FOOD
Army always have those courageous and good food only!

Examples of Superfoods:
- Fruits: Blueberries, strawberries, and cherries.
- Vegetables: Spinach, kale, and broccoli.
- Nuts and Seeds: Almonds, chia seeds, and walnuts.
- Other Superfoods: Yogurt, salmon, & sweet potatoes.

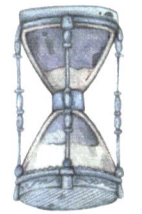

HISTORY PUNCH

ONCE UPON A TIME, in the Abbasid Caliphate, there was a village that cherished kale. They not only ate it but also believed it had healing powers. The wise scholars of the empire grew kale and used it for medicinal purposes.

One day, a young boy named John fell ill with a terrible stomach ache. His mother, Elizabeth, remembered the ancient tales of kale's benefits. She picked fresh kale leaves, boiled them, and made a simple broth.

As John drank the warm broth, Elizabeth told him, "The scholars of our caliphate believe kale can cure many illnesses, especially digestive issues." By the next morning, John felt much better. Amazed by kale's healing power, the villagers began using it as a remedy for various ailments, especially stomach problems.

The tradition of using kale for its health benefits was passed down through generations, making it a treasured part of their culture, celebrated for its miraculous properties.

Imagine you have a secret power-up button that you can press whenever you eat something super healthy. That's what superfoods are like! Every time you eat blueberries, it's like pressing a button that makes your brain super smart.

When you munch on spinach, it's like turning into a superhero with super strong muscles. Superfoods are delicious and fun ways to make sure your body has all the amazing powers it needs to be the best superhero you can be!

WHY ARE THEY IMPORTANT FOR YOU?

SUPER-FOOD

YOUR PRECIOUS BODY

Imagine your body like a castle, and superfoods are like knights guarding it and making it super strong.

HERE'S WHY THEY'RE SO IMPORTANT:

1. **Energy Boosters**: Superfoods give you tons of energy, just like how superheroes get their power from the sun or special potions. They help you run, jump, and play all day long without getting tired.

2. **Growth Helpers**: Like power potions for growing taller, superfoods have special stuff inside that helps you grow big and strong. They're like the building blocks for your muscles, bones, and brains.

3. **Health Defenders:** Ever heard of invisible shields? Superfoods have something like that—they protect your body from getting sick! They have special powers called nutrients that keep you strong and healthy, like a shield against bad germs.

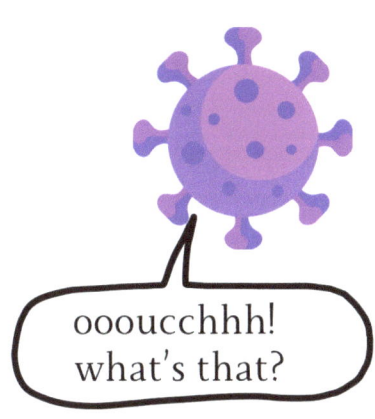

oooucchhh! what's that?

3. **Brain Boosters:** Want to be super smart? Superfoods can help with that too! They have special stuff that helps your brain think better and remember lots of cool stuff, just like how superheroes solve tricky puzzles.

SADLY, SUPERFOODS ARE LOST IN IT. CAN YOU HELP THEM?

Across:

2. An orange veggie that's sweet and great for your eyes.
3. A small, round, blue fruit that's great for your brain.
6. A creamy green fruit that's good for your heart.
9. A leafy green that makes you strong, like Popeye.

Down:

1. A tiny grain that's packed with protein and super nutritious.
2. A pink fish that's great for your brain and muscles.
4. A green veggie that looks like little trees and is super healthy.
5. A creamy snack that's good for your tummy.
7. A crunchy nut that's good for your energy and heart.

4. Heart Helpers: Just like superheroes protect the city from bad guys, superfoods protect your heart from things that might make it sad. They have special powers that keep your heart strong and pumping smoothly, so you can keep on being awesome.

5. Happy Makers: Eating superfoods can even make you feel super happy! They have things inside that make your body feel good, like getting a big hug from your mommy & daddy.

THANKS FOR SUPER-FOOD! I'M IN SUPER-SPEED!

5. Super Senses: Just like superheroes have super senses, superfoods can make your senses super too! They can help your eyes see better, your ears hear clearer, and your nose smell all the yummy smells around you.

The term "superfood" was coined in the early 20th century, during times of nutritional awareness and health campaigns.

8. **Mood Managers:** Superfoods aren't just good for your body, they're good for your feelings too! Eating them can make you feel super happy and ready to take on any adventure, just like your favorite hero in a comic book.

6. **Skin Superstars:** Ever wonder how mommies always have soft, glowing skin? Superfoods can help with that too! They have vitamins and stuff that make your skin super healthy and shiny, just like mommy's gentle touch.

Small Packet, Big Bang: Did you know that some superfoods are like tiny superheroes in disguise? Take chia seeds, for example! They may look small, but when you add them to your breakfast, they pack a punch that gives you the energy to zoom around like the Flash all day long!

9. Immune Boosters: Superfoods are like a shield that protects your body from getting sick. They have special powers that help your immune system fight off bad germs, so you can stay strong and healthy all year round.

Superfoods are like your personal team of helpers, giving you the energy and strength to tackle whatever comes your way. Think of them as your power-up, ensuring you never run on 'low battery' mode again! So let's pick our foods wisely and get ready to live our best, most energetic lives!

Are you ready to solve this jumble!

1. NGMAO _____

Soft and juicy, with a sweet and sunny taste that makes you smile with every bite!

2. WKII _____

Fuzzy on the outside, but inside it's juicy and tangy, like a tropical adventure for your taste buds!

3. GREAON _____

Bright and citrusy, with a juicy burst of tangy sweetness that's like sunshine in every bite!

4. WTBEYRSRAR _____

Juicy and sweet, with a little tanginess that makes your mouth water with joy!

5. WTEROAMLEN _____

Refreshing and crisp, with a juicy sweetness that's like a splash of happiness on a hot summer day!

6. AEILEPPNP ----------

Juicy and tropical, with a perfect balance of sweet and tangy that's like a burst of sunshine in your mouth!

7. NANABA ----------

Creamy and smooth, like a fruity hug in every bite!

8. CPHAE ----------

Soft and juicy, with a sweet and slightly fuzzy texture that's like biting into a slice of summer!

9. RPAEG ----------

Small and juicy, with a satisfyingly sweet taste that's like nature's candy!

Fruits

Welcome to the amazing world of fruits, where every bite is a burst of flavor and a boost of superpowers for your body! Fruits are nature's candy, packed with vitamins, minerals, and antioxidants that keep you strong, healthy, and ready for any adventure. Imagine a rainbow of delicious treats that not only taste yummy but also give you energy to play, think and grow. **Did you know that some fruits have super secrets?** For example, apples float on water because they are 25% air!

Watermelons aren't just tasty; they can be over 90% water, making them the perfect snack to keep you hydrated on hot days. And kiwis, those fuzzy little fruits, have more vitamin C than an orange, helping you stay strong and healthy.

HISTORY PUNCH

The Explorer's Superfood

Did you know that ancient explorers used to carry cranberries on their long sea voyages? In the 1700s, sailors packed cranberries on their ships because these tart berries could help prevent a disease called scurvy, which comes from a lack of vitamin C. Cranberries were like little red lifesavers, keeping the sailors healthy and strong during their adventures across the ocean. Imagine sailing the high seas with a stash of super berries to keep you safe and healthy!

Each fruit has its own special abilities. Some help your heart stay healthy, others make your brain sharp and many give your immune system the strength to fight off nasty germs. Ever heard of a fruit that can make your bones strong? That's right! Pineapples contain manganese, which helps build strong bones. Whether it's the crunch of an apple, the juiciness of a watermelon, or the tangy taste of a kiwi, fruits are here to make eating healthy fun and exciting. Let's dive into the fruity forest and discover some of these superfoods that are ready to power you up! Get ready to meet your new fruity friends and learn how they can make you a super-strong, super-smart, and super-healthy hero!

BLUEBERRIES

1.**Brain Boosters**: Blueberries are packed with antioxidants that help keep your brain sharp and improve memory. Eating blueberries can help you do better in school and remember things more easily!

2.**Heart Helpers**: These tiny berries are great for your heart. They can help lower bad cholesterol and keep your blood vessels healthy, which means your heart stays strong and happy.

3.**Eye Enrichers**: Blueberries have vitamins that are good for your eyes. Eating them can help you see better in the dark.

4.**Immunity Improvers:** They boost your immune system, helping you fight off colds and stay healthy. So, the next time you feel a sneeze coming on, reach for some blueberries.

5. Energy Enhancers: Blueberries give you energy to play and run around. They have natural sugars that provide a quick boost without any crash.

Rich in Nutrients: These berries are a good source of dietary fiber, vitamin C, vitamin K, manganese, and iron. They are one of the few fruits indigenous to North America that we still eat today.

Blueberries have been a crucial part of Native American diets for centuries. They were used in a mixture called pemmican, which combined dried meat, fat, and blueberries to provide a long-lasting, nutritious food source.

STRAWBERRIES

Hey there! Did you know that strawberries are not just delicious but also super healthy? Let's dive into the berry world and discover why these little red fruits are so amazing!

1. Boosts Your Brain Power- Strawberries help your brain work better. They have special nutrients called antioxidants that keep your brain sharp and help you remember things. Imagine doing better on your school tests and remembering all your favorite stories!

2. Keeps You Strong and Active- Strawberries are packed with vitamin C, which is great for your immune system. This means you'll get fewer colds and can play outside more often. They also help your body repair itself when you get hurt.

3. Great for Your Heart- These berries are good for your heart. They have fiber and antioxidants that keep your heart healthy and strong. Eating strawberries helps your heart pump blood better, making you feel more active and lively.

> A Fragile Fruit
> Strawberries are very delicate & need to be handled carefully. They don't ripen after being picked, so they are harvested when fully ripe. This makes them special and sometimes tricky to transport

A BERRY THAT'S NOT A BERRY!

Here's a fun fact: strawberries aren't actually berries! In scientific terms, they are called "aggregate fruits" because they come from a flower with many ovaries. This makes them different from true berries like blueberries and bananas.

4. Beautiful Skin and Shiny Hair- Vitamins in strawberries protect your skin from the sun and keep it smooth. They also help your hair grow strong and shiny.

Over 600 Varieties
There are more than 600 varieties of strawberries grown around the world. Each type has a unique flavor, size, and shape. Some are sweeter, while others are more tart.

5. Helps You See Clearly- Strawberries are good for your eyes. They have vitamins that protect your eyes and help you see clearly. Eating strawberries can help you spot things from far away and read your favorite books without straining.

6. Helps You Grow- Strawberries have important nutrients that help your body grow. They are full of vitamins and minerals that make your bones strong and help your muscles develop. Eating strawberries can help you grow tall and healthy.

The Strawberry Museum
There is a museum dedicated to strawberries in Belgium called "Le Musée de la Fraise." It showcases the history and uses of strawberries, and even has a strawberry-themed shop.

Strawberries are not just yummy; they are super good for you! They help your brain, heart, skin, eyes, and even help you grow. So, next time you see these red, juicy berries, remember all the amazing things they do for your body. Go ahead and enjoy some today – they truly are "Berry Awesome!"

STRAWBERRIES IN SPACE!

Strawberries have even been to space! NASA has included them in the food supplies for astronauts because they are nutritious and easy to store.

AVOCADOS

Hello there! Have you ever tried the creamy, green goodness of an avocado? This special fruit is not just yummy but also super healthy. Let's dive into the world of avocados and find out why they're called green gold!

1. Brain Fuel- Avocados are packed with healthy fats that your brain loves. These fats help you think faster and remember more. Eating avocados can make you a better learner and a memory master!

AVOCADO TREES CAN LIVE LONG

Avocado trees can live for hundreds of years. Some avocado trees in Mexico are believed to be over 400 years old and are still producing fruit.

2. Heart Hero- Avocados contain special fats and potassium that keep your heart strong and healthy. They help your heart beat perfectly and stay happy.

Popularity Boom: Avocados became widely popular in the United States only in the last few decades. The "avocado toast" trend and increased awareness of health benefits have made them a staple in diets.

3. Energy Enhancer- The healthy fats and fiber in avocados give you lots of energy. They keep you active and playful all day long, perfect for sports and fun activities.

NUTRIENT POWERHOUSE

Avocados are packed with over 20 different vitamins and minerals, including potassium (more than a banana!), folate, vitamin K, vitamin E, and B vitamins. They also have healthy fats that are good for your heart.

4. Strong Growth- Avocados have proteins and other nutrients that help build strong muscles and bones. Eating avocados helps you grow tall and mighty, ready to take on any challenge.

5. Happy Tummy- The fiber in avocados helps your digestive system work smoothly, keeping your tummy happy. It helps prevent tummy aches and keeps everything in balance.

Avocados are not just delicious; they have an interesting history and unique features. Let's uncover some rare and fascinating facts about where avocados come from, their history, and what makes them so special.

WHY ARE BLUEBERRIES CALLED BRAIN BERRIES?

Once upon a time, in a miraculous forest, there was a tiny village called Berryville. In Berryville, every berry had its own special power. There were strawberries that made your heart happy, raspberries that kept your tummy healthy, and blackberries that gave you glowing skin. But there was one berry that stood out above the rest—the blueberry, known as the "brain berry."

One day, a curious little squirrel named Sammy decided to find out why blueberries were called brain berries. Sammy loved adventures and solving mysteries, so he packed his tiny backpack with some nuts and set off to visit Wise Old Owl, the smartest creature in Berryville.

When Sammy reached the giant oak tree where Wise Old Owl lived, he called up,

"Wise Old Owl, can you tell me why blueberries are called brain berries?"

Wise Old Owl hooted softly and flew down to Sammy. "Ah, blueberries," he said, "they are indeed special. Let me tell you their story."

"Many years ago," Wise Old Owl began, "the berries of Berryville noticed that the forest animals who ate blueberries seemed to be the quickest learners and had the best memories.

The rabbits remembered where they hid their carrots, the deer could always find their way home, and even the tiny ants built the most intricate tunnels. The other berries were curious and decided to find out what made blueberries so special."

> HEY MY BERRY CLUB, WHY ONLY BLUEBERRIES ARE SO POPULAR, LET US SEARCH!

"As the berries investigated, they discovered that blueberries were packed with antioxidants,

HMMM... WHAT IS ANTIOXIDANTS, SO HARD TO EVEN SPELL?

Easy peasy, they are little helpers that protect the brain from damage and keep it healthy.

They also found that blueberries helped increase blood flow to the brain, giving it more oxygen and nutrients, just like a refreshing drink of water on a hot day."

"But here's the twist," Wise Old Owl said with a twinkle in his eye. *"One day, a strong wind blew through the forest, causing all the animals to become forgetful and confused. The wise blue elderberries, who were the leaders of the blueberries, shared their secret power with everyone.*

They made a special blueberry drink and gave it to all the animals. As soon as the animals drank the special drink, their memories returned, and they became even smarter than before."

"From that day on, everyone in Berryville called blueberries the 'brain berries,' and they became the most treasured fruit in the forest."

Sammy's eyes widened in amazement. "Wow, I had no idea blueberries were so powerful! Thank you, Wise Old Owl. I'm going to tell all my friends about the brain berries!" And with that, Sammy the squirrel scampered back to Berryville, eager to share the incredible story of the brain berries with everyone he met. From then on, all the animals made sure to eat plenty of blueberries to keep their brains sharp and their minds strong.

Now, you know kiddo why to take blueberries in your diet and one real fact is that:

> REGULAR CONSUMPTION OF BLUEBERRIES HAS BEEN SHOWN TO IMPROVE GENERAL COGNITIVE FUNCTIONS, INCLUDING REASONING AND DECISION-MAKING ABILITIES!

BERRY SMOOTHIE RECIPE

COLLECT THESE:
- 1 cup of mixed berries (fresh or frozen)
- 1 banana
- 1 cup of milk (or any milk substitute)
- 1 tablespoon of honey (optional)

FOLLOW EACH POINT:
- Put the mixed berries, banana, and milk into a blender.
- Blend until smooth.
- Taste and add honey if you want it sweeter.
- Pour into a glass and enjoy!

This smoothie is yummy and gives you lots of energy to play and learn!

VEGETABLES

Hey there, future champions! Did you know that just like you need special skills to be strong and smart, your body needs certain "power-ups" to stay healthy and full of energy? These power-ups come from something amazing called vegetables! Following are importance:

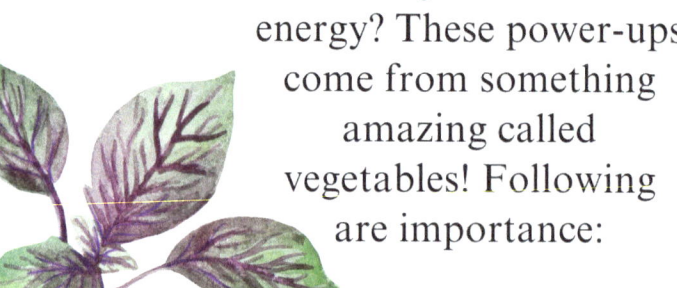

1. Energy Boosters: Vegetables give your body the fuel it needs to run, jump, play, and learn. Think of them as your secret energy source that helps you keep going all day long.

2. Super Strong Defenders: Vegetables are packed with vitamins and minerals that act like tiny bodyguards. They protect you from getting sick and help your body fight off any bad guys (germs) that try to make you feel unwell.

3. Brain Power: Eating vegetables can help your brain work better. They make it easier for you to concentrate, remember things, and think creatively. It's like giving your brain a superpower boost.

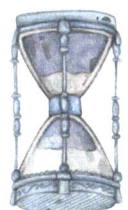

HISTORY PUNCH

The Tale of Kale: From Humble Beginnings to Superfood Fame

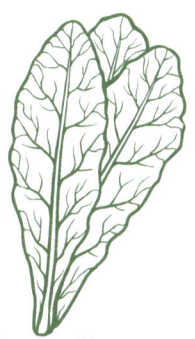

Once upon a time, in ancient Greece and Rome, people loved eating a leafy green vegetable called kale. It was known for its incredible health benefits and was even believed to give strength to soldiers. Fast forward to the Middle Ages, and kale became a common vegetable in European gardens. It was easy to grow and survived in cold weather, making it a reliable food source during tough times.

During World War II, the British government encouraged people to grow kale in their gardens to ensure they had enough nutritious food despite the shortages caused by the war. This initiative was called "Dig for Victory." Kale became a symbol of resilience and health.

However, after the war, kale fell out of favor and was often used just as a garnish on plates. But kale's story didn't end there! In the early 2000s, health experts began to rediscover its amazing nutritional benefits. People started calling it a "superfood" because it was packed with vitamins, minerals, and antioxidants. Kale made a huge comeback and became a trendy food, featured in everything from smoothies to salads.

Today, kale is once again celebrated for its health benefits, showing that sometimes, the simplest foods can be the most powerful.

SPINACH

Spinach is a leafy green vegetable that is often called a "superfood" because it is packed with important nutrients that help our bodies stay healthy. Here's why spinach is so great:

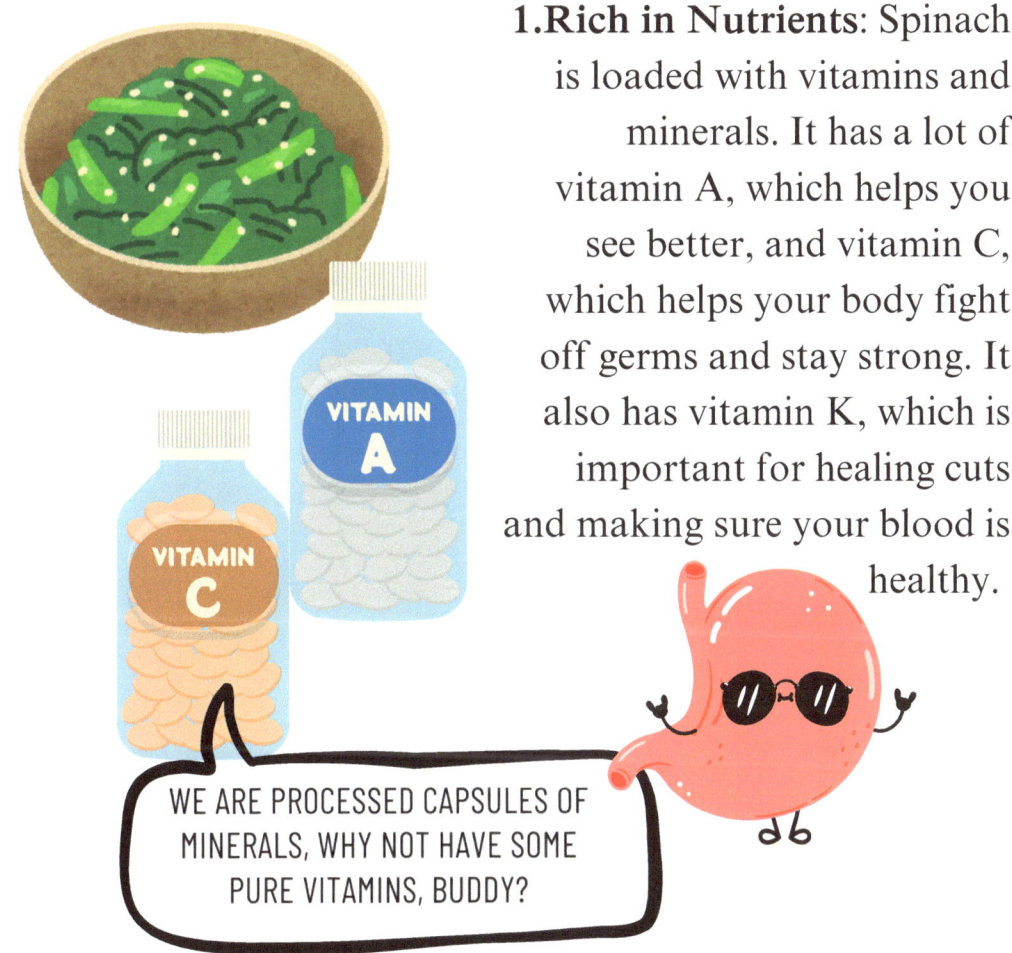

1. Rich in Nutrients: Spinach is loaded with vitamins and minerals. It has a lot of vitamin A, which helps you see better, and vitamin C, which helps your body fight off germs and stay strong. It also has vitamin K, which is important for healing cuts and making sure your blood is healthy.

WE ARE PROCESSED CAPSULES OF MINERALS, WHY NOT HAVE SOME PURE VITAMINS, BUDDY?

2. Good for Digestion: Spinach is high in fiber, which helps your tummy digest food properly and keeps everything moving smoothly. This means less tummy aches and more happy meals.

3. Strong Bones: Spinach contains calcium and magnesium, which are essential for building strong bones and teeth. This means eating spinach can help you grow up with a sturdy skeleton.

4. Healthy Blood: Spinach has a lot of iron, which is necessary for making red blood cells. Red blood cells carry oxygen around your body, giving you energy to play and learn.

5. Brain Power: The folate in spinach is great for your brain. It helps your brain work better and can even improve your memory. This makes spinach a brain-boosting food.

KALE

Hey there! Got bored! Let's talk about kale, a leafy green vegetable that is super healthy and why it's called a superfood.

VITAMIN K
VITAMIN A
VITAMIN C
FIBER
ANTIOXIDANTS

1. Packed with Nutrients: Kale is filled with vitamins and minerals that help your body stay strong. It has a lot of vitamin A, which is great for your eyes, and vitamin C, which helps you fight off colds and heal faster.

2. Powerful Antioxidants: Kale contains antioxidants, which are like tiny warriors that protect your body from getting sick.

They keep your cells healthy and can even help prevent some serious illnesses.

3. Strong Bones: With lots of vitamin K and calcium, kale helps build strong bones and teeth, so you can run, jump, and play without worries.

4. Good for Skin and Hair: The vitamins and minerals in kale help keep your skin glowing and your hair strong and shiny.

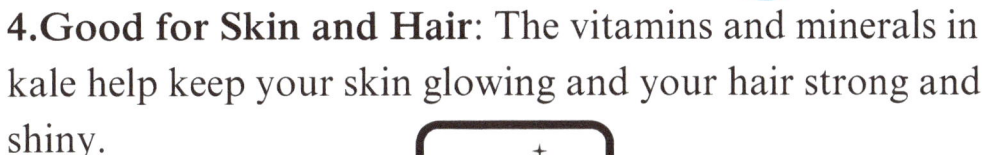

5. Healthy Heart: Eating kale can help keep your heart healthy by lowering bad cholesterol and providing fiber, which is good for your tummy and heart.

Old Vegetable, New Fame: Kale has been around for over 2,000 years! Even though it seems like a new trendy vegetable, people have been eating it for centuries.

Super Nutrient-Packed Award

We will assign different awards to outstanding superfood among all, here goes the second award!

*It has **more calcium than milk** and **more vitamin C than an orange**. Plus, it's loaded with vitamin A and omega-3 fatty acids, which are great for your brain & eyes.*

Secret recipe from kale!

Caution:
- **Supervision**: Always have an adult help with the oven and cutting.
- **Hot Surfaces**: Be careful with hot baking sheets. Use oven mitts!

Ingredients:
- 1 bunch of kale
- 1 tablespoon olive oil
- A pinch of sea salt

Instructions:
1. **Preheat the Oven**: Set your oven to 300°F (150°C).
2. **Prepare the Kale**: Wash the kale thoroughly and dry it well. Remove the thick stems and tear the leaves into bite-sized pieces.
3. **Season the Kale**: Place the kale pieces in a large bowl. Drizzle with olive oil and sprinkle with sea salt. Toss to coat evenly.
4. **Arrange on a Baking Sheet**: Spread the kale pieces in a single layer on a baking sheet lined with parchment paper.
5. **Bake**: Place the baking sheet in the oven and bake for about 20 minutes. Check them at 15 minutes to ensure they don't burn. They should be crisp but not brown.
6. **Cool and Enjoy**: Let the kale chips cool for a few minutes before eating. Enjoy your homemade, healthy snack!

SWEET POTATOES

Sweet potatoes are an awesome vegetable that you can eat in many ways! Here are some fun and cool reasons why sweet potatoes are great for you:

1. Strong Immune System: They have lots of vitamin C, which helps your body fight off colds and illnesses. It keeps your body strong and healthy.

2. Strong Bones: They have calcium and manganese, which are important for building strong bones. This helps you grow tall and strong.

3. **Super Eyesight**: Sweet potatoes are packed with vitamin A, which is great for your eyes. It helps you see better in the dark and keeps your eyes healthy.

4. **Energy Boost**: Sweet potatoes give you lots of energy because they are rich in carbohydrates. This means you can run and play without getting tired quickly.

5. **Healthy Digestion**: They have plenty of fiber, which is good for your tummy. Fiber helps food move through your body and prevents constipation.

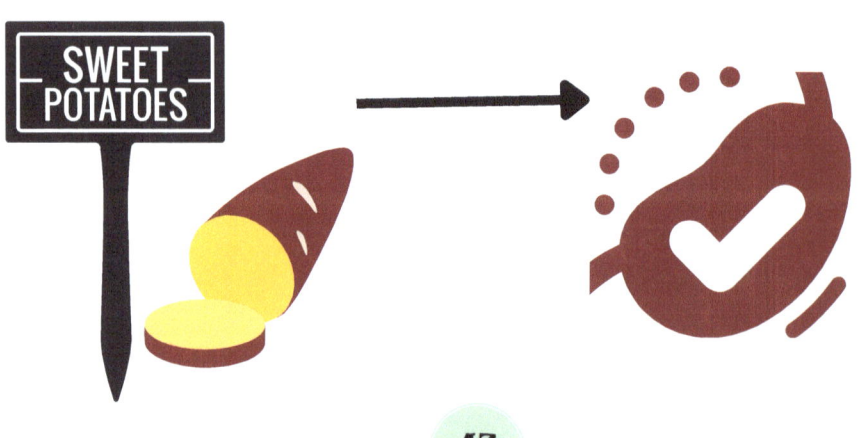

CARROTS

Carrots are not only crunchy and tasty but also packed with nutrients that help your body grow strong and healthy. Here's why carrots are a fantastic superfood:

1. Great for Your Eyes: Carrots are rich in vitamin A, which helps you see better, especially in low light. This vitamin is essential for preventing poor vision and night blindness.

2. Boost Your Immune System: Carrots contain antioxidants, which help protect your body from getting sick. These antioxidants keep your immune system strong and healthy.

3. Strong Teeth and Gums: Carrots are good for your teeth too! Chewing raw carrots helps clean your teeth and gums, making them stronger and healthier.

Hey Rabbit! No more secret! I know now reason behind your famous two teeth health secret. Hehehe....

3. Healthy Skin and Hair: Eating carrots can help keep your skin and hair looking great because of their high levels of vitamins and minerals, like vitamin C and potassium.

5. Good for Digestion: Carrots have lots of fiber, which helps keep your digestive system working well. Fiber is important for preventing constipation and keeping your tummy happy.

```
R O W T S Q D S I Z A K A O E
E G T I O S X L W C Y X S F M
W K M A I R O H K E P V T V V
O D U K M C R C H R E P P E P
L F O P C O T A O T U T S O U
F T V O V S T N C E D W D O J
I Y R R T X B I O F D J F S H
L B K A L E L P W O T Z L N Q
U Q Q O L F O S M L D V V Q F
A C M L G X B X V B I J P T I
C B I J E K L O Q H J S O S B
F S D W T T M T S R B H T G V
K R G C P I J L R D Y T A R Y
U D G Q J M V T L I N I T H T
V O M I T C B B R C H F O A L
```

Bell Pepper
Cauliflower
Sweet Potato
Tomato

Broccoli
Kale
Spinach
Carrot

WHAT MAKES CARROTS GOOD FOR YOUR EYES?

FUN FACT

Once upon a time, in a quaint village, there was a wise old farmer named Eli. Eli was known far and wide for his lush, vibrant vegetable gardens. Among all his crops, the carrots were the most famous. They were bright orange, incredibly sweet, and seemed to glow in the sunlight. One day, a group of curious children visited Eli's farm. They loved playing in his fields and often helped him with his gardening chores. One of the children, a boy named Sam, asked, "Farmer Eli, why do people say that carrots are good for our eyes?" Eli smiled and gathered the children to make a circle and surround her. "Let me tell you all a story," he said. Many years ago, when Eli was a young farmer, he traveled to a distant land to learn new farming techniques.

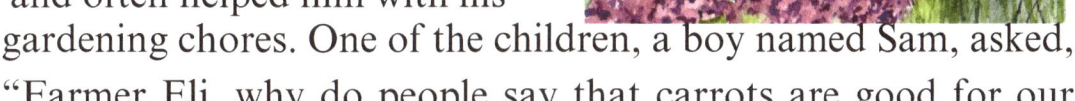

In a far-off desert, he met an ancient tribe known for their extraordinary eyesight. They could see far into the distance, spotting travelers and animals long before anyone else. Eli was amazed and asked the tribe's elder, a woman named Asha, how they had such incredible vision. Asha took Eli to a secret garden hidden deep within desert. There, he saw fields of the most sparkling carrots he had ever seen, their bright red tops peeking out of the rich soil. "These carrots are our secret," Asha explained. "We have grown them for generations, and they are filled with a special nutrient called beta-carotene. When we eat these carrots, our bodies turn the beta-carotene into Vitamin A, which keeps our eyes healthy and our vision sharp."

Eli was fascinated and asked if he could take some seeds back to his village. Asha agreed, and Eli returned home with the precious seeds, eager to share his newfound knowledge. But as soon as Eli returned to his village,

"Vitamin A is a nutrient that helps keep your eyes healthy and helps you see better in the dark. It's like food for your eyes, making sure they work well and stay strong."

"Think of beta-carotene as a tiny, invisible helper inside carrots and other colorful veggies. When you eat a carrot, the beta-carotene travels inside your body to your liver, where it's miraculously transformed into vitamin A. This super nutrient then rushes to your eyes, helping you see better in the dark and keeping your eyes healthy. So every time you munch on carrots, you're powering up your eyesight!"

he faced an unexpected problem. The soil in his village was very different from the rich, dark soil of the desert garden. Eli planted the carrot seeds with hope, but the carrots grew small and pale, not vibrant like in the desert. Eli was puzzled and worried. The villagers were eager to see the miraculous carrots he had promised. Not wanting to disappoint them, Eli decided to do something different. He started experimenting with different ways to enrich the soil. He added compost, rotated his crops, and carefully tended to his garden every day. After many months of hard work and patience, Eli's efforts paid off. The carrots began to grow strong and bright orange

and red, just like in the desert garden. When the first harvest came, he shared the carrots with everyone in the village, explaining their special powers.

Over time, the villagers noticed that their eyesight improved, especially at night. They could see clearer and farther than ever before. The children were amazed and loved hearing about Eli's hard work and determination. Sam asked, "But how do carrots actually help our eyes, Farmer Eli?" Eli explained, "Hmm Sam you know carrots are full of beta-carotene, which our bodies turn into vitamin A. Vitamin A helps our eyes stay healthy by keeping the surface of our eyes, called the cornea, in good shape. It also helps us see better in dim light. That's why eating carrots can help you see better, just like the tribe in the desert." And so, the secret of the wise old farmer's miracle carrot fields spread far and wide. People from distant lands came to learn from Eli and grow their own carrots, ensuring that everyone could benefit from the gift of clear sight.

So, the next time you crunch on a carrot, remember the tale of Farmer Eli and the miracle carrot fields. Carrots truly are good for your eyes, helping you see better and keeping your vision strong. It's not a magic—just the wonderful power of nature and a bit of miracle from the highest, creator of me and you!

 "The cornea is the clear, front part of your eye that covers the colored part and the black center (the pupil). It helps your eye focus light so you can see clearly."

SPINACH OMELET RECIPE

Ingredients:
- 2 eggs
- A handful of fresh spinach leaves (about 1/2 cup)
- 1 tablespoon of milk
- Salt and pepper (just a pinch of each)
- 1 tablespoon of butter or oil
- Optional: shredded cheese (like mozzarella)

Instructions:
1. **Prepare the Spinach:**
   - Wash the spinach leaves thoroughly to remove any dirt or grit.
   - Pat them dry with a paper towel.
2. **Beat the Eggs:**
   - Crack the eggs into a bowl.
   - Add the milk, salt, and pepper.
   - Whisk everything together until it's nicely mixed.
3. **Cook the Spinach:**
   - **Caution:** Turn on the stove with adult supervision. Heat half the butter or oil in a small frying pan over medium heat.
   - Add the spinach and cook for 1-2 minutes, just until the leaves wilt. Remove the spinach from the pan and set it aside.

4. **Make the Omelet:**
    - **Caution:** Handle the pan carefully; it's hot. Add the remaining butter or oil to the pan.
    - Pour the egg mixture into the pan, tilting it to spread evenly.
    - Let the eggs cook for a minute until the edges start to lift from the pan.

5. **Add Spinach and Optional Cheese:**
    - **Caution:** Avoid touching the hot pan. Use a spatula for safety.
    - Spread the cooked spinach evenly over the half of the omelet.
    - Sprinkle cheese over the spinach if using.

6. **Fold and Finish:**
    - Carefully lift one edge of the omelet and fold it over the spinach.
    - **Caution:** Make sure to use the spatula to avoid direct contact with the hot surface.
    - Cook for another minute or until the bottom is golden and the cheese melts (if used).

Serve:
   - **Caution:** Let the omelet cool for a few minutes before cutting or eating to avoid burns.
   - Slide the omelet onto a plate.
   - Enjoy your delicious spinach omelet!

Tip: You can add a little more flavor by sprinkling some herbs like chives or parsley on top before serving. Always have an adult nearby to help with the cooking!

QUINOA

Quinoa is a fantastic food that's packed with nutrients. Here are 8 benefits of quinoa explained for your goodness:

1. Super Protein: Quinoa has lots of protein, which helps our muscles grow and stay strong.

Cool Colors
Quinoa comes in different colors, including white, red, and black, and each color has a slightly different taste and texture.

2. Full of Fiber: Fiber in quinoa helps our tummies digest food and keeps us feeling full longer.

3. Brain Food: Quinoa has nutrients that are great for our brains, helping us think better and do well in school.

ANCIENT SUPERFOOD
Quinoa has been eaten for thousands of years and was a staple food for the ancient Incas in South America.

4. Energy Booster: The carbohydrates in quinoa give us lots of energy to play and learn all day.

5. Bone Strengthener: Quinoa contains calcium, which is essential for building strong bones and teeth.

6. Immune Support: The vitamins and antioxidants in quinoa help boost our immune system, so we stay healthy and can fight off colds and other illnesses.

Grows in Harsh Conditions
Quinoa plants can grow in tough environments, like high altitudes and dry areas, making them very resilient.

7. Mineral Rich: It's packed with important minerals like magnesium and potassium that keep our bodies healthy.

8. Easy on the Tummy: Quinoa is gluten-free, which makes it gentle on our stomachs and good for kids with gluten sensitivities.

CHIA SEEDS

Chia seeds are tiny, but they pack a lot of goodness. Here are 8 cool benefits of eating chia seeds: Ready? Go!

1. Packed with Energy
Chia seeds are like little energy boosters. They help keep you active and ready to play because they provide a lot of nutrients in a small amount.

Chia seeds are packed with antioxidants that help protect your body from free radicals, which can cause cell damage. These antioxidants contribute to slowing the aging process and maintaining overall health.

2. Strong Bones:
Chia seeds have lots of calcium, which is important for building strong bones and teeth, just like drinking milk.

3. Fiber Fun: They have a lot of fiber, which helps your tummy feel full and keeps your digestion running smoothly.

Despite being so nutritious, chia seeds are low in calories. Just one ounce has only 137 calories but is packed with essential nutrients.

4. Brain Boost

Chia seeds are rich in omega-3 fatty acids, which are great for brain health and help you think clearly and learn better.

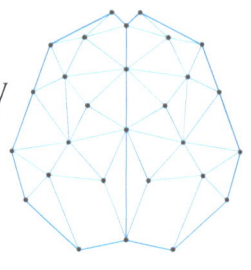

PROTEIN POWERHOUSES

Unlike many plant-based foods, chia seeds are a complete protein, meaning they contain all nine essential amino acids that our bodies can't make on their own. This makes them an excellent protein source, especially for vegetarians and vegans.

5. Mighty Muscles

They provide protein, which is essential for building and repairing muscles, making you stronger.

6. Happy Heart

Eating chia seeds can keep your heart healthy because they have nutrients that support good heart health.

7. Gel-Forming Fiber: Chia seeds contain a type of soluble fiber that forms a gel in your stomach. This not only helps you feel full for longer, which can aid in weight management, but also helps to slow down the absorption of sugar into your bloodstream, providing a steady energy release.

Oats might look like tiny grains, but they pack a punch when it comes to making you healthy and strong. Let's dive into why oats are such an awesome superfood for you!

1. Energy Boosters: Oats give you lots of energy to play and learn. Oats are also excellent brain food. The steady energy from oats helps your brain stay focused and alert, so you can concentrate better in education.

PREHISTORIC OATS

Evidence suggests that people in Switzerland were eating oats as far back as 32,000 years ago! Long before oat milk became popular as a dairy alternative, ancient civilizations like the Egyptians and Greeks made oat-based drinks. They would soak oats in water, strain them, and drink the nutritious liquid.

2. Tummy Helpers: Oats have something called fiber, which is like a broom that helps clean out your tummy. This keeps your digestion smooth and helps you feel full, so you don't get hungry too soon.

3. Heart Protectors:
Eating oats helps keep your heart healthy. They have a special type of fiber called beta-glucan that helps lower bad cholesterol, which is good for your heart.

> **STEEL-CUT VS. ROLLED**
> Steel-cut oats are chopped into pieces, while rolled oats are steamed and flattened. Both are healthy, just prepared differently!

NATURAL DYE
In some cultures, oats were used to create natural dyes for fabrics, giving them a beautiful, earthy color.

4. Better Sleep:
Oats can help you sleep better because they contain melatonin and complex carbohydrates that increase the production of serotonin, a chemical that helps you relax and sleep well.

5. Glowing Hair: Oats are rich in iron and zinc, which are great for keeping your hair healthy and shiny.

HEALING OATS:
In various cultures, oats were used in traditional medicine. For example, ancient Chinese medicine used oats to help with digestive issues, while European folk remedies used oat baths to soothe skin irritations.

Space Oats: Did you know that oats have even been considered for space missions? Scientists believe that oats are a great food for astronauts because they are nutritious, easy to store, and provide long-lasting energy. Oat-based meals can be an excellent option for space travelers on long missions.

6. Boosted Athletic Performance: The energy and nutrients in oats can help you perform better in sports and physical activities, giving you that extra boost when you need it.

7. Stable Mood: Oats help keep your blood sugar levels stable, which means your mood stays more even, and you're less likely to feel grumpy or tired.

ECO-FRIENDLY CROP

Oats are considered a sustainable crop because they require less water and fewer pesticides compared to other grains. This makes them an environmentally friendly choice for farmers and consumers alike.

Horse Power: Before oats became a human superfood, they were mainly used to feed horses. Horses loved them for the same reasons we do—they give lots of energy!

8. Calm Nerves: Oats have magnesium, which can help keep your nerves calm and your muscles relaxed.

Oat straw (the stalks left after harvesting oats) is used as bedding for animals. It's soft, absorbent, and keeps animals comfortable and dry, making it a preferred choice on many farms.

9.**Strong Muscle Builders**: Oats have proteins that help your muscles grow strong. If you like running, jumping, or playing sports, oats can help you get better at them.

Oats are not just good for you; they're good for the soil too! Planting oats can improve soil health by preventing erosion and adding organic matter back into the earth. Farmers often use oats in crop rotation to maintain healthy fields.

WHY ARE CHIA SEEDS A SUPER SEED?

FUN FACT

Once upon a time, in the vast, sunny landscapes of Mexico, there were tiny seeds considered so valuable that they were used as currency. These were not ordinary seeds; they were chia seeds, known today as a super seed.

Long ago, the Aztec warriors carried small pouches filled with these seeds. Before a long journey or a big battle,

they would eat just a spoonful. Why? Because chia seeds were believed to give them high energy and endurance, which was crucial for warriors. Now, here's where our story takes an interesting twist. Fast forward to today, scientists decided to study why these tiny seeds were so valued by the Aztecs. What they discovered was truly surprising! They're also full of fiber, protein, and calcium. All these nutrients are essential for keeping our body strong and healthy.

So, from being a warrior's secret weapon centuries ago, chia seeds have now become a favorite healthy snack for people all over the world. And that's why we call chia seeds a super seed, not because they have magical powers, but because they're a powerhouse of nutrition, strong enough to fuel an army and smart enough to keep us healthy in modern times.

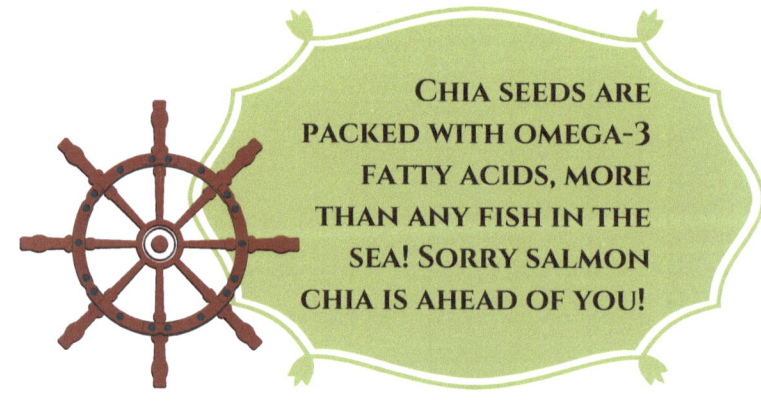

CHIA SEEDS ARE PACKED WITH OMEGA-3 FATTY ACIDS, MORE THAN ANY FISH IN THE SEA! SORRY SALMON CHIA IS AHEAD OF YOU!

QUINOA SALAD RECIPE

Collect these:
- 1 cup quinoa
- 2 cups water
- 1 cucumber, diced
- 1 tomato, diced
- 1/2 red bell pepper, diced
- 2 tablespoons olive oil
- 2 tablespoons lemon juice
- Salt and pepper to taste

Instructions:
1. **Cook the Quinoa:**
   - Ask an adult for help with the stove. Rinse 1 cup of quinoa under cold water.
   - Put quinoa and 2 cups of water in a pot. Bring to a boil, then simmer for 15 minutes until fluffy. Let it cool.
2. **Prepare the Vegetables:**
   - Wash and chop the cucumber, tomato, and red bell pepper into small pieces.

3. **Mix Everything Together:**
    - Put cooked quinoa and chopped vegetables in a bowl.
    - Add 2 tablespoons each of olive oil and lemon juice.
    - Sprinkle salt and pepper to taste.
    - Mix gently.
4. **Serve and Enjoy:**
    - Let it cool a bit before eating. You can keep it in the fridge to chill.
    - Enjoy your yummy quinoa salad!

Tip: You can add other stuff like cheese or beans or herbs if you like. Just have fun making it your own!

SALMON

kiddo, have you ever heard of it? It's not just any fish. Let us dive into the world of salmon and discover why it's so special!

1. Brain Boosting Omega-3s: Salmon is loaded with omega-3 fatty acids, which are like super fuel for your brain. They help you think clearly, remember things better, and even feel happier!

2. Strong Bones and Muscles: Did you know that salmon is full of protein? Protein helps your muscles grow big and strong, and it also keeps your bones healthy and sturdy.

3. Healthy Heart: Eating salmon helps keep your heart strong and healthy. Those omega-3s we talked about? They also help lower the risk of heart disease and keep your heart pumping strong.

4. Sharp Eyesight: Salmon is rich in a special nutrient called vitamin D, which is great for your eyes. It helps you see clearly and keeps your eyes healthy and shiny.

CHICKEN

Hey kids, have you ever wondered why chicken is such a popular food all around the world? Let's explore the wonderful world of chicken and discover why it's a superfood that's great for your body and mind!

1. Power Packed Protein: Chicken is like a superhero when it comes to protein! Protein helps your body to grow a strong figure with muscles, so you can run faster, jump higher, and play enough. It's high-protein can promote feelings of fullness and that prevents overeating.

GLOBAL SUPERSTAR

Chicken is one of the most popular meats in the world, enjoyed by people from all corners of the globe. In fact, there are more chickens on Earth than any other bird species!

2. Strong Bones and Teeth: Did you know that chicken is full of a special mineral called phosphorus? Phosphorus is like a secret agent that sneaks into your bones and teeth, making them super strong and tough. Regular intake of phosphorus through foods like chicken helps maintain bone density and dental health. Phosphorus is vital for muscle function and repair, making it important for active individuals and athletes.

bone check!
bone check!

ROYAL ROOSTERS

Chickens were one of the first animals to be pets for food by humans, way back in ancient Mesopotamia, around 6000 years ago!

People started keeping them for their tasty eggs and later discovered how delicious their meat was too. Even kept as pets by kings and queens. They were even featured on ancient coins and sculptures as symbols of wealth and power.

3.Energy Boosting B Vitamins: Chicken is rich in B vitamins, like B6 and B12, which are like little energy boosters for your body. They help turn the food you eat into energy, so you can keep going and going like the Energy Bunny!

4.Happy Hearts: Eating chicken can make your heart smile! It's low in unhealthy fats and high in good stuff like omega-3 fatty acids, which keep your heart healthy and strong.

Super All-Around: Chicken is like a culinary chameleon—it can be cooked in so many different ways! From crispy fried chicken to savory chicken soup, there's a chicken dish for every occasion and taste bud.

5. Feathered Recycling Machines: It can eat leftover food scraps from your kitchen, turning waste into eggs and meat. They are like natural recyclers that help reduce food waste. Chick loves to peck and scratch at the ground, which helps keep gardens and farms clean by eating bugs and pests. They are like tiny helpers that keep the environment healthy and balanced.

ANCIENT ANCESTORS

Did you know that chickens are descendants of wild jungle fowl that lived in the forests of Asia thousands of years ago? They were much smaller and looked quite different from the chickens we see today!

6. Science Helpers: Chickens are often used in scientific research to help us learn more about health and diseases. By studying chickens, scientists can discover new ways to keep both animals and people healthy.

AMAZING EGGSHELLS

Chicken eggs are incredibly strong! In fact, the average egg can withstand about 90 pounds of pressure on its long axis. That's like putting the weight of a small child on top of a single egg without breaking it!

NUTS

Have you ever wondered why squirrels love nuts so much? Well, it turns out they're onto something! Let's crack open the world of nuts and discover why they're not just tasty treats but also superfoods that give us lots of energy and keep us healthy.

1. **Super Snack Energy:** Nuts are like little energy boosters packed with nutrients! They're full of healthy fats, protein, and fiber, which give you lots of energy to play, run, and have fun all day long.

Oops! Almonds Aren't Nuts: Technically, almonds are seeds of the almond fruit, which grows on trees. True nuts, like acorns and chestnuts, have a hard shell that doesn't split open naturally.

2. **Brainy Boosters:** Did you know that nuts are great for your brain? They're loaded with important nutrients like vitamins and minerals that help your brain think clearly, remember things better, and stay sharp.

Nuts have iron, which helps carry oxygen in your blood to your brain. More oxygen means your brain can send and receive signals faster, making you quick and sharp, just like a lightning bolt!

We can't stop here! Nuts also contain zinc, which helps your brain stay focused and sharp. It's like a special fuel that keeps your mind clear and helps you concentrate on your homework or favorite book.

3. Healthy Skin: Nuts are rich in vitamin E, which is like a secret potion for your skin! Vitamin E helps keep your skin soft, smooth, and glowing, so you can shine like the full moon.

4. Environmental Benefits: Nuts are a sustainable food source that requires fewer resources like water and land compared to animal-based foods. By choosing nuts as a snack or ingredient, you're helping to protect the planet for future generations.

Peanuts Are Legumes: Despite being called nuts, peanuts are actually legumes, like beans and lentils. They grow underground, unlike most nuts that grow on trees.

5. Reduced Risk of Allergies: Studies have shown that early exposure to nuts can help reduce the risk of developing nut allergies later in life. Eating nuts in moderation can help train your immune system to tolerate them safely.

Kiddo! Do you have any allergy? No. Then have your nuts to prevent it and stand strong.

6. Boosted Energy Levels: Nuts contain natural sugars and healthy fats that provide a quick energy boost when you need it most. Snacking on nuts can help keep you fueled up for all your adventures.

Nut Trees Live Long: Some nut trees, like the pecan tree, can live for over 200 years. Imagine a tree that's older than your great-great-great-grandparents, still producing delicious nuts!

7. Stable Blood Sugar: Nuts are low in carbohydrates and have a special kind of fat that helps keep your blood sugar levels steady. This means you won't get those ups & downs in energy & mood, keeping you feeling balanced and happy.

HOW DOES SALMON HELP YOUR BRAIN?

FUN FACT

Once upon a time, in a small coastal village nestled between the mountains and the sea, there lived a curious boy named Alex.

Alex loved to explore and learn new things, but he often found it hard to concentrate and remember everything he discovered. His grandmother, Nana Elsa, a wise woman with a twinkle in her eye, noticed his struggle and decided to share an ancient secret with him. One breezy afternoon, Nana Elsa called Alex to the kitchen, where a delicious aroma filled the air.

She was cooking a dish that Alex loved: grilled salmon. "Sit down, Alex," she said with a warm smile. "I want to tell you a story about this wonderful fish and its miraculous powers."

Long ago, in a village much like their own, the people were known for their wisdom and sharp minds. They could solve complex problems, invent useful tools, and remember stories passed down through generations. People from distant lands often visited to seek their advice and knowledge.

Curious travelers would ask, "What is the secret to your incredible brains?" The villagers would always smile and point to the sea. "It's all thanks to the salmon," they would say. Alex leaned in closer, his eyes wide with interest. "Salmon?" he asked. "How can a fish make you smart?"

Nana Elsa chuckled and continued. "In those days, there lived a wise elder named Seraphina who wanted to understand why salmon had such a profound effect on their minds. She observed the salmon closely and discovered that these fish were rich in something called omega-3 fatty acids." Alex furrowed his brow. "Omega-3 fatty acids? What are those?"

Nana Elsa explained, "Omega-3 fatty acids are special nutrients that help your brain work better. They strengthen the connections between brain cells, making it easier to think clearly, remember things, and learn new information. It's like giving your brain a powerful tool to do its job well."

As Seraphina shared her findings, the villagers began to include salmon in their meals more often. They noticed that not only did they feel more alert and focused, but they also had better memories and could think more creatively. Word of their discovery spread, and soon, people from all around started to eat more salmon to boost their brainpower.

Alex's eyes sparkled with excitement.

"So, eating salmon can really help me think better and remember more?" he asked.
"Yes," Nana Elsa replied.
"Salmon is a superfood for your brain. It's full of healthy fats, vitamins, and minerals that keep your mind sharp and your body strong."
From that day on, Alex looked forward to his salmon dinners, knowing that each bite was not only delicious but also helping his brain grow and thrive. He began to notice that he could concentrate better on his homework, remember facts from his favorite books, and even come up with new ideas for his school projects.

And so, the secret of the smart salmon continued to be passed down through generations, helping young minds like Alex's grow stronger and brighter, all thanks to the miraculous power of this incredible fish.

CHICKEN WRAP RECIPE

Ingredients:
- 1 cooked chicken breast (shredded)
- 2 whole wheat tortillas
- 1 cup shredded lettuce
- 1/2 cup diced tomatoes
- 1/2 cup shredded cheese
- 1/4 cup creamy salad dressing

Instructions:
1. Prepare Ingredients & CAUTION: Ask an adult for help when using a knife to dice tomatoes and shred lettuce.
2. Mix Chicken:
    - Combine shredded chicken with a little ranch dressing (creamy salad dressing).
3. Assemble Wrap:
    - Lay a tortilla flat. Spread some ranch dressing (creamy salad dressing) in the center.
    - Add shredded lettuce, diced tomatoes, shredded cheese, and chicken.
4. Roll Wrap:
    - Fold sides in, then roll up tightly from the bottom. Do the same with the second tortilla.

    Enjoy your tasty chicken wraps!

Most people are brought up believing that if they are a good person, good things will happen to them. While not entirely wrong, it's not enough to unlock your potential. It's like walking up to a door with two locks and only one key. If you want to go inside, you need the other key. The second key is going positive and going first—proactively helping others. When both keys are used together, the door unlocks, and a previously hidden world of opportunities reveals itself.

–FS

In upcoming launch it will be variety, including an encyclopedia for kids on Entrepreneur!

UNIQVISE

is my initiative to spread authentic and simplified informations in an unique and to the point talks. I am an university student and looking forward to change myself and elevate the condition of current chaotic world with the help of the Creator, the one! Catch me at instagram account: "shahab_an_initiative".

www.ingramcontent.com/pod-product-compliance
Lightning Source LLC
Chambersburg PA
CBHW041433010526
44118CB00002B/64